A
Series
of
Beautiful
Collisions

Sammi Walker

BookWise Publishing, Riverton, Utah.
bookwisepublishing.com

Cover Image and Design by: Chris Walker
Editor: Joshua Brothers
Interior Design by: K Christofferesen

ISBN 978-1-60645-273-8   Paperback

Library of Congress Control Number: Pending

10 9 8 7 6 5 4 3 2 1

12/1/2020

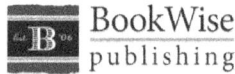

BookWise
publishing

A NOTE TO THE READER

A book of poetry is never intended to be wolfed down in a single sitting.

Rather, you should treat this book like the old pillowcases used on Halloween nights, slung over our backs and digging into our shoulders, the lumpy contents bulging against the tight cotton weave. Returning home, we each had our own little hiding place for such treasure. Each night, you should fish this book of poetry out from your secret cache, select a few morsels to eat, and leave a small trail of wrappers behind you, evidence of your delight plastered across your face.

This collection of poetry is an accurate reflection of a living soul. I have had the privilege of watching Sammi grow as a writer and as a human being over the past five years, and have been touched with the depth, honesty, and clarity with which she explores her unique human experience. As she continues forward in life, as do we all, I am confident that her powers wielding the written word will only grow stronger, and she will become a voice for her generation.

You will be tempted, but do not gobble up this book too quickly.

Pick a few. Savor them after a night toiling in the dark.

Read them after you have taken your mask off and can truly enjoy the gifts gathered for you as Sammi has traveled from house to house: gifts that are now freely given to you.

Joshua Brothers
December 2020

CONTENTS

LOVE

BODY

CHILDHOOD

MIND

GET TO KNOW THE AUTHOR

ABOUT SAMMI

MY HONEST POEM

HE was a city rose, disguised by house smoke.
SHE was a land star, who bounced from puddles to windows.
SHE thrived in the dark,
HE ached for the sun.

THIS IS FOR THAT ONE PART IN THE MOVIES
WHERE THE TWO BACKGROUND CHARACTERS FALL IN LOVE
AND THERE'RE NO CAMERAS AROUND TO SEE IT.

Picture this:

The main characters have just walked out of the restaurant

They stop in front of the door

While he tucks her hair behind her ear

Space Song by Beach House is playing in the background

And their lips touch for the first time

And it is raining

But they are under an awning

So she doesn't get her hair wet

Their faces lit by passing cars

And that

Is where we come in

The background characters

Only a passing car to you

But for us

The windows are down

And it is still raining

Hair is soaked already

Radio is blasting *Electric Love* while my head is hanging out of the sun roof

And he looks at me as if he is seeing a sunset for the first time

—cue the montage—

We are making our way around the city
Empty streets
And halo lights
Knowing every word to every song

And this
Is the love story they try to show you
This "I've known you for years" kind of connection
But they miss the fact that it's not about the crowds

It's about
How one night can feel like minutes
But your connection has felt like forever

And maybe at first we didn't want to be the background characters
But you fall in love for the night and forget in the morning
While we are up till 6 am drinking cherry cola
Realizing that the stars are brighter without a spotlight

SOMETHINGS TO KNOW BEFORE DATING ME PART 1

After Jamie Martara

1. My lungs are too good at pick up lines, so if you walk into the room, it's best if you know CPR because even with all these inhalers you still take my breath away.

2. I will never get a degree in small talk, so let me show you the universe.

3. If you have ever said hi to me, it's best to assume you are shoved somewhere in this book.

4. I keep my font size at 2 so it's easier for you to talk over.

5. I hate my name. I shortened it from 22 letters to 5 because I've never filled someone's whole mouth and felt like I've belonged there.

SOMETHINGS TO KNOW BEFORE DATING ME PART 2
A LITTLE LESS POETIC BUT A LITTLE MORE REAL THAN PART 1

1. I will show you every song that makes me think of you and see how long it takes you to figure out what lyrics are attached to your name.
2. Any sentence starting with the words "You should" followed with "this food" will ALWAYS end badly for you.
3. I talk with colors.
4. I don't know how to communicate otherwise.
   But that's why this poem exists.
   I struggle to keep eye contact.
5. I love the way the stars talk.
6. If I could invent a candle smell it would be a mixture of wet pavement and crushed up daisies.
7. Any poem I show you was edited twenty more times just because I knew you would see it.
8. I will always be bad at talking because I can't edit it twenty times before you hear it.
9. If I'm not replying, it's because I'm sleeping.
10. I will always eat fries even if I say I don't want them.
11. I'm usually quiet if my brain is too loud.
12. Every poem I will ever send will be for a reason; you just have to figure out what line I've tied your name to.

TO THE BOY WHO WORKS AT STARBUCKS

After Rudy Francisco

To the boy who works at Starbucks . . .
I like your smile, it's as if Arm & Hammer had a flashlight and used
Morse code to get my attention. Maybe, Colgate turned to Cupid and
accidentally shot a coffee-covered arrow into my heart and now I can't help
but drizzle when I see your smile.

To the boy who works at Starbucks . . .
Hi . . . Can I get your numb—a caramel macchiato? I don't drink coffee, but
I'll buy one everyday just to talk to you. Because I really do like you . . . a
latte.

To the boy who works at Starbucks . . .
Your coffee-ground colored eyes make my insides swirl like cream in a fresh
cup; I wanna taste your brown sugar kisses. I wanna espresso these feel-
ings, but all I have are these puns.

To the boy who works at Starbucks . . .
I promise I'm not a stalker; I just have a really hard time talking to
people . . . like you. So I keep buying drinks, and when it gets to the point
where you ask if I want the "usual," I will laugh, roll my eyes, and say,
"Bean there, drank that," hoping that this joke will break the ice, and I can
sugarcoat this question with a dollop of whipped cream.

Before I can get this question out, I see you lock lips with a "Skinny latte," her skin so vanilla. My anger foams, and before I know it, I'm drowning myself in coffee. Week after week, drink after drink. White teeth become stained with an addictive hue.

To my caramel macchiato . . .
This started as a first item friendship and has developed into a caffeinated relationship. Days without you leave me feeling empty, and I'm in need of a refill.

To my steaming hot espresso . . .
Your diabolical aroma fills the room, your bitter-taste sweetened by a white chocolate mug, and with each sip I get deja brew.

To my cappuccino . . .
To my Americano . . .
To my skinny mocha . . .
To my . . . To my . . .
To my decaf days . . .
Scatterbrain thoughts blend together like whipped cream and hot drinks, headaches vary throughout the day, and I often find myself pro-caffein-ating. Hands trembling like blenders slowly getting faster.

To the boy who worked at Starbucks . . .
I hope that "skinny latte" treats you well, and by the looks of it, things are going just fine with that ring that's looped around her finger, caramelized in diamonds.

JUKEBOX HERO

I want to sit with you in a cold basement. Speakers maxed out drinking Beyoncé's lemonade. Throw in a bit of Ariana's sweetener and give it a lil' mix.

I will be your jukebox hero while we listen to the chain smokers outside the window; while they breathe language into their lungs with each evaporated verse.

Our hands, will dance into each other the way fingers twist around bass strings. Twist until they break. Until they bleed. Twisted to perfection.

Our magnetic kisses will turn to cassette tape tongues. Wound around warped records. Breath turned to needles following grooves between skin. Carving deeper with each loop of this turntable. Round and round until the room is spinning.

And I don't know if I'm more nauseous from the spinning, or the heavy smell of alcohol. But as soon as my lyrics lump in my throat, you turn my teeth to quarters. Plucking them from my mouth as if they were unwanted; as if they were just there for you to take.

She has become your jukebox hero. You, her coin collector. Showering her with my earnings to replay her voice over and over again.

I pretend it doesn't hurt. That you are using my silver to feed into your jukebox lover.

So she can serenade you with her sweet, sweet words. Drowning out my suffering until my words become the hands that pluck at my vocal cords like broken bass strings in the background of your love song.

Scrapping her too, you left us both to gather dust in your murky basement. Not leaving a single piece behind. So you could take long drives with your new pop princess or your jazz blue babies. Your choices were endless in your new hot rod. Your life became the highway, and you had no destination. But you stopped at every exit on the way.

From AM to FM they came in waves, Mrs. MP3 to Mrs. CD.
You tried them all, Leaving them just as fast as you could pick them up, one after the other. Until one day you ditched your rambunctious radio love for something more intimate.

You didn't just want to listen anymore; you wanted to hold the words. Control what they would say; so you found yourself a digital Delilah who followed you from New York to LA.

But I, a rusted record player, once the color of your summer sunburns, have started to bubble and peel long after you. Leaving me without my beloved casing, followed by a dulled needle. Covered with a dust blanket, crawled on my ear worms. I'm now looking for a new playlist to cancel out that one-hit wonder.
That one touch.
That one smell.
That one taste.
That last loop . . . That last loop . . . That last loop . . ..

I HOPE . . .

I hope every time it rains you think of me.
I hope every drop is a reminder
That you just can't get off your skin.
I hope you sit outside
And wish for the rain to hold you;
I hope it never feels like I did.

I hope you think the only way to get me off your mind
Is to sleep.
I hope that I am your bedsheets only dream;
I hope you wake up every time
They mumble my name into your pillow.

I hope your next girlfriend also writes poetry.
I hope you tell her her poems are full of lies
Before you find yourself in every line.

I hope my profile pops up on the
"People you may know" page daily
So you are always reminded
Of what you could have had after I have moved on.

IDEA:
MOVE AS IF PIECE BY PIECE
YOU'RE LETTING GO OF EMOTIONAL BAGGAGE
AND WATCH YOURSELF FRAGMENT.
ALLOW YOURSELF TO TURN
A JAGGED EDGE IN AN ELASTIC BODY.

HIP BONES

Hello hip bones

Hello exposed bones

Hello double-decker skeleton

Tour bus bones

Hello hand magnets

Mine and his

Both for different reasons

Hello reflection in dressing room mirror

Hello dented hourglass

Hello new bikini

Hello less confident

Home reflection

Hello swimsuit receipt

Hello high waisted jeans

88°

Hello hip bones

CLOSE ENOUGH TO SEE IT

This is an ode for my eyes.

Not for the ones that are mud-colored or the ones infused with chocolate. This is for the eyes that are the color of sun pushing through full bottles of whiskey; for the eyes that are the color of the earth after it rains.

When I was born, I was a black-haired blue-eyed baby. My eyes were never a bright ice, more of a dull denim. The best way to describe them would be . . . the perfect pair of mom jeans found at the thrift store. They were already worn and loved by someone else; they've seen things long before my time.

But I am not a blue-eyed kinda girl. I figured that out six months into this world, so they changed. The same way seasons do, slowly. It took six months for my eyes to melt into April afternoons, the kind of afternoons that make kids' shoes dirty when splashed in.

This is an ode for my eyes.

My eyes have watched hot days squeeze the life out of Popsicles; seen ants try to run from the sticky river of sugar that drips from my cousin's hands.

My eyes have seen the way 4th grade kids kick up gravel when they run, and the way their hair flies when they fall.

This is an ode for my eyes.

The ones that were boxed in at age 10, watched behind thin glass as my grandma's fingers tried to hold onto this world until my grandpa got there; they watched as he didn't make it in time.

My eyes have learned to hold onto tears; they've learned that glasses clear vision, not sight. They've learned to scream when my mouth couldn't. My eyes have been loved, then forgotten, just to be loved again; my eyes have been burned too many times.

But this, this is an ode for my eyes.
The eyes that were made to have two sides. From far away my eyes are empty; they are endless puddles of still pen ink. Those are the eyes most people see.

But up close they hold recipes. They are the color of homemade pancakes under thick syrup, they will stick with you like a rich caramel, and remind you of a hickory glaze, all outlined with a hint of lime. You just have to be close enough to see it.

This is an ode for my eyes.
The ones that know there's more to the world than Bible verses and rock arches; they just have yet to see it. My eyes want to be sand sifters, to look at every grain that no one else appreciates; to be microscopes in a world of telescopes because they know the little things make the bigger picture.

But my eyes still want to know how old the stars are, to travel back in time to see how they were made. My eyes want to read every handwritten poem, watch the way the letters flow, how hard they are pushed into the paper. Because you can read the worst pain in the happiest words, you just have to be close enough to see it.

KRAKEN

To be a myth is to spend your whole life non-existing, to live in the mouths of others.

To be a myth is to be talked about but not talked to; lonely days are spent wishing for monsoons, rough seas and tired sailors.

It's waiting for waves of wooden ships big enough to hold because this ten-ton body has been a written folktale.

To be a folktale is to be a hand-me-down, to be changed and added to. Who is going to love a creature of my size?

A monster with eight arms and a mouth that has only known how to crush every story that is told too close because it did not wish to called Kraken, or to take up this much room.

Sailor, why do you sink under so much body? My lonely one shouldn't be too much of an anchor because there is only one of me.

But, I mean, if your body was big enough to hold four-and-a-half whaler ships' worth of people's stories, you too would be saturated in enough emotion to make you baggage.

Since my first ship, I have envied every captain for choosing to stay on a sinking vessel. When everyday I wish to jump overboard.

Captain, why do you fear me? Is it because the ocean turns to black ink on a clean page before I surface? Maybe it's because according to you, this Kraken craves flesh that is live and elastic.

I have taken dozens of your sailors, wrapped up eight at all at once, and I sank. Their eyes melted into darkness, and water anchors their lungs. Only few have survived me.

But it's not my fault they haven't adapted to the oceans pressure and lack of oxygen, eventually we all get pulled down from the monstrous weight . . .

SILENT DEATH

Breathe.

Press me
Against your lips,
Wrap them around me
Inhale me
I will take you away,
Slowly

Breathe.

I am addiction rolled in your death certificate.
My breath is poison,
I will never love you,
But I will wait.
Wait for you to cough up lava;
And when your lungs harden into magma,
And you are being suffocated by your own ashes
I will watch.
Watch your insides erupt,
Watch until your very existence is extinct.

I have turned your body into a museum.
It's full of everything from brown teeth,
To petrified air.
Black walls covered in soot,
You're a museum only I would want to visit.

Breathe.

I am an illusion,
An embalmer,
I started mummifying you from the first kiss,
Draining the air from your body,.
And you,
Knowing this was possible,
Continued.

Breathe.

Fill your mouth with another coffin nail,
And exhale me.
The day you try to get rid of me
Will be the day you realize you can not live without me.
When you put me down,
And your breath becomes invisible,
Though I no longer twist and curl around your eyes,
Your body will remain burned.

Breathe.

The day you try to get rid of me will be the day you realize
My ghost will continue dancing through your body forever.
You will realize I am your cremator,
And that your ashes mean nothing when they are tinted yellow.

Breathe.

You will realize
Your whole world could fit in a rolled up strip of paper.

Breathe.

That a marionette can be controlled by two fingers.

Breathe.

I have grown to know you;
I have gone with you
To the alleyway behind every movie,
The corner of each barbecue and birthday party;
I have grown so fond of you.

But remember,
This is not a love story.
You came to me.
Pressed me against your lips,
Wrapped them around me,
Inhaled me.
And I took you away.

Slowly.

So . . .

Breathe.
Just.

Breathe.

THIS BODY

I wish my body had never forgotten how to move.
I wish it remembered how to depart like fallen angels
Before the collapsing of their wings.
I wish I could withdraw my whole self
From this gravity.

I wish these arms remembered how to tangle,
And this skin knew how to lunge and plummet and parachute.
I wish these legs remembered how to leap,
And how to catch this body gracefully.

I wish I remembered how to write prompts with just music and these limbs.
I wish this body danced
As if piece by piece I was dropping emotional baggage.
Letting it fall from me with a purpose,
Knowing I would never need it again.

But instead,
This body is stagnant;
This body is gray tones and stuttered movements ;
This body hesitates every motion;
Walks like a broken echo;
Or a balled up reflection.

This body is an apologetic fragment;
A mournful scrap of this creation
Of this composition—
This architecture.

This body loves like arthritis;
This body pleats like a letter
In a crowded envelope,
Never able to flatten itself out again

This body wants to be a combination
Of symmetrical lines
And proportionate rhythm .
This body wants to stop teeter-tottering
Its way around the right moves.
This body wants to stop pleasing
Anyone but itself.

This body wants to remember what it's like to scream
In silence.
This body wants to remember addiction
Shoot this body up with melody;
Numb it with acoustics
Until we are hypnotized
By the motion.

LET'S DIG UP THE STREETS
AND FILL THEM WITH SKY,
SO WE CAN SPLASH IN CLOUDS
INSTEAD OF RAIN.

THAT CHILDHOOD SMELL

It's July 4th,
And my childhood home is up in smoke.
Children are hiding in the garden
With the only light coming from booming backyard fireworks.

Glow sticks are scattered through the lawn;
The tree house is still dripping from water balloons.

The rocking chair is full of a t h i n n i n g man
with a rounded stomach.
He is staring at an ashtray on the fireplace that now
holds more ash than the urn it replaced.

SWEET TASTE OF HEAVEN

Some days
I wonder what heaven tastes like.
If it's still ice cream on back patio swings,
or muffins on a Sunday morning.

Other days I wonder
how the bathroom is still coated in your perfume.
I wonder how pillows feel after seven years of grief and cigarettes.
I wonder if the rocking chair still tries to hold you.

Most days
I know you are still needed,
in the garden,
in the soil,
in the tree house.

All of these days
I wonder why you were plucked first.
I wonder if the world grabbed fistfuls of your hair
as it snaked from your head
down shower drains,
thinking that it could re-root 67 years of Italian curls,
or endless melodies.

A lot of days I think about your last.

I wonder if your lungs tried to make room for the air,

tried to pull in what was last of home.

I wonder what your words were,

what my words were,

what color were eyelids when forced into coma.

I wonder

how many days I will never remember we had.

I wonder what heaven tastes like today.

DOORWAYS

In my life,
I've been dealt a handful of doorways.
So many that I couldn't tell you what knob
Or color the first one had.

I've moved so many times that
Yellow became blue, and blue became red;
And I wish there were walls for all these primary colors.

Keypads turn heavy metal in my pocket,
Too loud to forget about and too heavy to lose.

What I guess I'm trying to say is
My life is a shell game,
And I don't know what roof I'll be hiding under next.

I want to know what it's like
To walk on a globe
That isn't spinning out
From beneath my feet.
And it'd be nice
If my GPS knew where I was.

But I find the sink drain comforting
Because the water goes down the same way;
A rapid whirlwind my eyes can't seem to stray from.
It must be nice
to be water;
To always know which way to go,
Even if it's only down.

I ask my boyfriend, is it nice?
To have your life be so constant?
Is it nice
To know what reflection you're gonna see
When you look into the mirror?

Or to be able to say your name and age
without saying umm before you answer.

I guess what I'm trying to say is . . .
I miss the comforting whispers of a gray room;
I miss the days where the smell of coffee would crawl in bed with me.
That meant the sun was about to stutter through the blinds.

I find it funny
We used to say my house was made of porcelain,
And the people caring for me told ME not to fracture it,
When in reality they were the ones with wrecking-ball bodies
And mouths like wood chippers.
I was left hanging from the scaffolding.

A lot of days
I miss the way I could sift through comfort like sand;
Let it slide between my fingers,
knowing that I could never run out.
When everything around you is always moving,
it's really easy to feel like you're alone.

But then I remember
there are 93 kids at my school who are "homeless" too;
Transient teens,
Never in the same place twice.
These kids aren't just stick and handkerchief;
They aren't just paper cups
on a blackened street
or cardboard signs.

We are the backpack children
Who want family dinners,
And pancakes in the morning,
Or even a room to clean,
We want everything that will never fit in our bags
And the luxury of taking our bed sheets for granted.

ROTTING ROOTS

My dad was only 9 when his pancreas decided to divorce his body
and stop paying for child support.
He woke up most nights high,
wrist deep in too much sugar.
Other nights,
Grandma found him sleepwalking in the backyard
by the fence that gave splinters for kisses.
The night she found him shuffling down the street
is the same night she added countless locks to the door.

Every day since it's been:
a little low,
sleep walk,
test strip,
beeping blood checker.
A little high,
needle,
measure,
insulin shot.

His mother was 40
when she contracted type 2 pancreatic failure.
His father followed with type 1.
But it's fine;
my family is always having shots with dinner.
My grandpa,

Half failing liver always has 2 shots . . .
an hour,
cheers to his father
and his father before that
for a never-ending chain of Bailey's Coffee lovers.
That's his secret for staying so thin.

I'm just a branch on a tree
Where breaking glass vials and needles are life-threatening;
Where sometimes the sun is too much for one branch
And others stop growing too soon.
When I was born,
my mother's mother contracted cancer.
Both the cancer and I grew together;
the only difference was
I lived past 10.

After we lost my grandma's branch,
We all lost a little bark.
That day, my grandpa inhaled addiction,
forced it down his lungs
and invited it to live with him.
Now his leaves reek of grief.

The doctor
diagnosed this family tree years ago,
and I guess it's fine because
My body always fails to feel good anyway;
but if I were every disease that branched from this tree,
I would be everything but body.

My lungs,
colon,
breasts,
and bones
would be cancer infested.

My body,
a breeding ground for disease;

My skin,
A Dalmatian with too many sun spots;

My lungs,
Cotton-padded, keeping second-hand smoke from bleeding in;

My heart
Screams doctor, doctor hand me that pacemaker
because the left branch would be heart attack,
and the right, stroke.

The truth is . . .
If I was every disease that branched from this tree,
I would never learn how to wither from the top down
because my roots were planted rotten.

LAY YOURSELF IN MY STARS
AND DRIFT INTO DARKNESS

RAIN

When rain hits a surface, it stretches itself out as far as it can to take in as much of the world as possible before returning to the clouds.

And oh, to be rain.

To not just run your hand across the Earth but to be a part of it. To cuddle with the concrete and reflect the city lights. To land upon your skin, or your clothes, or your lips.

To be rain, is to be a storyteller, is to collect colors through condensation so we can put them in the sky. To be rain, is to teach the clouds how to bleed in apricot and wrap it in midnight to show them how beautiful they can be even though all of this pain.

To be rain, is to never be comfortable. Imagine, being rain. To be cursed for all of this growth but praised for all your vivid aches.

To be rain, is to always be let go; is to always be falling; is to land in something bigger than you and feel like you have lost yourself. Rain is not knowing what shape you started off as and being okay with it.

EVERY SHADE OF BLACK

he tells me, i remind him of the ocean; how i am every shade of blue in till black; how people think i'm only as deep as my surface but in reality i swallow problems the size of ships, downing gallons of ocean just to devour them whole. he asks me if i love the ocean.

no. confused, he asks why and i think;

think about how i'm constantly holding my breath, waiting and waiting for my face to break the surface. to fill my lungs with another gulp of air, to finally F E E L sun . . . but i am always an arms-length away from my next breath.

i wait and wait until my body shuts down. i think about how i let the water seep in through
my nose,
my mouth,
my skin.

i called this feeling empty claustrophobia. it's where my body has all the room to move, but i'm stuck inside my own skin, my own mind; thoughts take up most of the room; this feeling reminds me of swimming;

like when you first jump in the water on a hot day, how it makes the air bubble off your skin and out of your lungs; how it holds you and doesn't want you to leave.

this feeling is somewhere between calm and dying. i've been here before, but it still scares me every time. i think about how i can lose complete control of my body; how it starts at my fingers and continues until it numbs every inch of me, until i'm shaking. i called this "relaxed."

in a way, this is scuba diving; the way my body shakes against the waves, how the colder i get, the harder i shake. the harder i shake, the harder it would be to hold my head above the water.

it's like knowing you have an oxygen tank on your back, and not being able to get the mouthpiece in until the last second; knowing that this thing could save your life but yet weigh you down all at the same time.

i think about how many ways there are to drown. some ways i've known since elementary school. some are so unfamiliar to my brain it tracks the symptoms as if they were a new species of fish.

i remember all the shades of blue he talked about, and how on his blues scale i would feel better in black where no one could see me. i think about how dark it is at the bottom of the ocean; how many monsters live down there; how when i close my eyes i feel like i'm there.

pulling me out of my deep sea thoughts, he asks me once more:

why do you not love the ocean?

i reply: no one ever taught me how to swim.

THE SPECTRUM OF BULLYING

After Rylee Leonard

Shake the box,

Puzzle-piece girl.

Doesn't it sound nice?

A collection of pieces

Waiting to be artwork.

A yellow one here

And a purple one over there.

All of them,

Fragments of a greenhouse oasis.

The roses said:

"Your seeds were planted in poor soil."

"Your body was made poorly."

And a lot of days,

You feel like crying.

But,

The people who pull petals from flowers

Don't deserve the spring.

Don't let their barb

Keep the Berlin blue

From your pink harmony.

Listen,

The clouds cry too.

They scream

And rumble

And boom.

And even though they are tearful,

And you are terrified of rain,

It keeps you growing.

It calms the earth's colors

So the spectrum stays vibrant.

I would say,

Don't follow the roses;

Don't copy the pool

Of deep scarlet

And cliches.

Don't be the basic rose

When you can be a

Lotus or

A Poppy

Shake the box

Puzzle-piece girl.

Put it up to your ear.

Doesn't it sound nice?

Doesn't it sound like

Lullaby birds

And nights full of zodiacs.

Doesn't it smell like

Sweet pea,

4 o'clock,

And chocolate cosmos.

Girl,

Don't worry about your hands,

Or the things you will never be able to hold.

Cause this world is big,

And it's heavy,

And it's overflowing with hues.

And though

You can never be the gardener,

It doesn't mean you can't love the flowers.

There will be days

Where your shoulder angel and devil melt;

Where your autism and ADHD will liquefy.

And let me tell you right now,

Those days are hard.

But you—

You are not hated.

You are not defined by a difference.

You are not what a group of 10-year-olds say you are.

You told me yourself.

You are an Aries.

A confident,

Bold,

Bundle of curls.

Don't let a collection of

Cancers and Capricorns

Tell you how to write a poem.

Don't give them a page

Of your happiness.

VAN GOGH

Van Gogh,
Teach me how to hurt and make it beautiful.
Show me how up close insanity is just lines,
But from far away it is something worth showing.
Teach me how to coil stars
And wash over irises with indigo.
Show me how to watch the night sky through cafe windows,
Or learn to love the olive trees.

Paint me in oil,
A mixture of deep blues and muted yellows,
Show me the parts of myself that are worth painting.
Hang this version of me in a museum
And maybe, for once, I will believe in compliments.
You taught me that an artist will always lose bits of themselves,
But as long as they have their hands, they have something worth showing.

And you,
Vincent,
Showed this world how beautiful the view was from a gray-walled asylum;
Showed that though mania
Things still grew on your bad days.
You gifted this world color,
But all they saw were pen marks and brush strokes.
They could not see what you saw;
They were not ready for a mixed-media masterpiece.

So . . .

They took you away.

Called your mental illness self-destruction

When in reality it was just a good day for painting.

And you,

Canvas in hand,

Shoes in wheat,

Found yourself on the wrong side of a gun.

Found that bullets do not enter the body as pastel as you thought

But instead,

They barge through you;

No thought needed;

And soon . . .

There bleeds mahogany,

Followed by crimson,

And perian,

And brick,

And sangria,

And redwood,

And spice,

And amber,

And rust,

And . . . ivory,

And linen,

And salt,

And eggshell,

And cream,

And white,

And abalone,

And harbor,

And smoke,

And lead.

Van Gogh,

The day you were shot, the color drained from your body,

Though you couldn't hand the world your vibrance,

You did learn to tell them about it.

With the right amount of words you could create anything.

I use metaphors instead of paint brushes for my images;

I use certain sounds to sculpt your swirling skies.

We are not different . . .

You, a 1800s millennial,

And I, a trying adult.

Together we want to see the unthinkable,

Reaching for the stars we know we will hold;

So instead, we create them—

Keep them in our back pockets for the next time

The world tries to question us or our art.

You make art for the deaf,

And I the blind.

Teach me how to show them our masterpiece
And all of the colors they have never seen before.
Tell me all of the hues used for your imagination
So I don't get the language wrong.
Show me the difference between lilac and mauve,
Honey or amber,
Salmon or scarlet,
Maybe imperial.

We are not different . . .
We are just the artists waiting for the right audience
To paint a picture for.

IF TO LOVE A METAPHOR
IS TO LOVE MYSELF,
THEN I WANT TO BE ASH;
VOLCANIC,
BUT THE PEACEFUL PANIC
AFTER A DISASTER.

GET TO KNOW THE AUTHOR
MY HONEST POEM
AFTER RUDY FRANCISCO

I was born on October 30th;
That makes me a Scorpio,
Which is ironic because
I am a water sign that cannot swim.

I've never been in a haunted house;
I'm lactose intolerant;
5'6;
Spend more time with words,
Than I do with people.

I'm a little too obsessed with rain,
The color yellow,
And poetry.
(But together, they are a good mix.)

I've been told I have weirdly specific playlist names;
And I do.
But, they sound the best around 10 pm.
I will only listen to a new song for the first time
In my car with the windows down
And the seat back.

I am a pageant girl
Who has always loved science.
I thought I was going to be an astronaut,
But, instead I switched from stars to genes
Because to quote myself,
"The little things make up the bigger picture."
I'm guilty of writing more poems
About the parts of me I wish to fix,
Rather than the parts I like the most.

But, I am the best me with dark hair.
Cut just below my shoulders.
I am the best me when writing.
Preferably with a .5 pen in a black notebook
That has smudged pages and a cracked spine.

I spend a good portion every day
Reading poetry books
Because I'm always so jealous
Of the way others can put words together.

I am scared of blow-up Christmas balloons,
Tiny holes,
And objects that make me feel small.
That's probably why I won't walk under Jupiter
At the planetarium.

My biggest pet peeve is water on the counter;
I hate the word crisp.
And my body has never gotten along with food.

I will never understand why people like
Scary movies,
Christmas music,
And Justin Bieber.
I'm still learning a lot of things
Like how to keep my sneakers clean,
Sleep with the lights off,
Or how to end this poem.

ABOUT SAMMI

Sammi Walker is a teenage poet. She competed with her high school slam poetry team for three years before she graduated. Sammi now competes for the state of Utah and coaches high school students. Though Sammi's slam poetry started her sophomore year, she has been writing poetry since the 7th grade. She would like to thank Sue Wierman for introducing her to poetry. She would also like to thank Joshua Brothers, Karen Christoffersen of BookWise Publishing, and Steve Haslam; without them this book would have never happened.

www.ingramcontent.com/pod-product-compliance
Lightning Source LLC
LaVergne TN
LVHW051806080426
835511LV00019B/3425